Be Active

by Mari Schuh

Raintree is an imprint of Capstone Global Library Limited, a company incorporated in England and Wales having its registered office at 264 Banbury Road, Oxford, OX2 7DY – Registered company number: 6695582

www.raintree.co.uk
myorders@raintree.co.uk

Edited by Christianne Jones
Designed by Sarah Bennett
Original illustrations © Capstone Global Library Limited 2021
Picture research by Morgan Walters
Production by Laura Manthe
Originated by Capstone Global Library Ltd
Printed and bound in India

978 1 3982 0292 4 (hardback)
978 1 3982 0291 7 (paperback)

British Library Cataloguing in Publication Data
A full catalogue record for this book is available from the British Library.

Acknowledgements
We would like to thank the following for permission to reproduce photographs: iStockphoto: FatCamera, 13, 18, 21; Shutterstock: AlohaHawaii, 24, B Wright, 16, BlueSkyImage, 27, fizkes, 23, Golden Pixels LLC, 12, Iakov Filimonov, 29, Jose Gil, 17, michaeljung, 9, Monkey Business Images, 5, People Image Studio, 22, Photographee. eu, 11, photonova, Cover, design element, pixinoo, Cover, Rawpixel.com, 20, Rob Marmion, 8, Sergey Novikov, spread 14-15, Spotmatik Ltd, 25, TinnaPong, 7, Zurijeta, 19.

Every effort has been made to contact cop
this book. Any omissions will be rectified in
the publisher.

All the internet addresses (URLs) given in t
press. However, due to the dynamic nature
changed, or sites may have changed or cec
author and publisher regret any inconvenie
no responsibility for any such changes can
the publisher.

Contents

Bold words are in the glossary.

Move it

Have you moved your body today? Did you play outside at break time? Maybe you walked to school. Maybe you rode a bicycle.

Some kids enjoy football. Other kids like to skate. There are so many ways to be active! What is your favourite way to get moving?

Healthy and strong

Why is it good to move your body? It keeps you healthy and strong! It builds strong bones. When you are active, your lungs work harder. They take in more oxygen. This makes your lungs stronger. Exercise makes your heart strong too.

Being active makes your muscles strong and **flexible**. Your **balance** and **posture** get better when you are active. Exercise can also help you be a healthy weight.

Staying active feels good! Exercise gives you more energy. You might feel very happy. It may help you worry less.

People who are active often sleep better. But try not to exercise just before you go to bed. It might be hard to get to sleep.

Being active helps you in many ways. It can help you **focus**. You might have more energy to learn. Exercise also helps you feel better about yourself. It gives people **confidence**.

Get ready

Before you exercise or play, make sure you are ready. Take some time to warm up your body. Do some stretches. Take some deep breaths.

You might go to the doctor for a check-up. You will learn about your health.

Make sure you exercise safely. Always listen to your body. Exercise should not hurt. Stop if you are hurting. Tell an adult about it.

Kids should be active for at least one hour a day. Good news! You can do it in small parts. Maybe you play football at break. Then you swim after school.
It all adds up to one hour of exercise.

Set **goals** to move every day. Make plans to play with friends. Sign up for new sports. Limit your time on phones and computers. That will give you more time to play.

What you wear when you play is important. The correct shoes keep you from getting hurt. Ordinary shoes are not good for running. Old shoes can hurt your feet. Make sure you wear a helmet when you ride your bike.

If you play outside, think about the weather. A baseball cap will keep the sun out of your eyes. Wear suncream to protect your skin. Is it hot? You might want to wear shorts. Is it windy? Make sure you take a coat.

Playing sports

Sports are lots of fun. They are also a great way to be active. When you play a sport, you move your muscles. Your heart pumps. Your lungs work hard. Sports help keep your body fit.

What sport do you want to play? If you like to run, try basketball. Or you might like cricket. Do you want to play inside? Try **karate** or gymnastics.

Sports help you learn many skills. You
learn to follow rules. Sports teach
you how to play fairly. You also learn
about teamwork. Be a good friend
when you play. Cheer for others.
Be nice to all the kids on the team.

Don't want to join a team? You can play sports in other ways. Run with a classmate. Play catch with your family. Ask your friends to swim with you. Shoot hoops at home. Mix it up!

Be prepared when you play sports.
Make sure you have the equipment you
need. Wear your team uniform. Take
your water bottle. Get ready to play!

Take good care of your body. Warm
up before you are active. You might do
jumping jacks. Do a few arm circles.

After you play, make sure you stretch
gently. Stretch your whole body.
Breathe slowly and deeply. Make sure
you drink extra water.

Moving in many ways

Don't enjoy sports? No problem! There are many ways to be active.

You can exercise at home. Count how many sit-ups you can do. Then do a few push-ups. Try doing some **yoga**.

Don't want to miss your favourite TV programme? Exercise while you watch it! See how many jumping jacks you can do. Dance to music. Turn up the volume and have fun!

You don't have to go far to exercise outside. You can be active in your garden or park. Play in the leaves. Build a snowman. Play catch with a friend.

Get moving with your family. Ride
your bikes. Do a **scavenger hunt**.
Go for a hike. Walk your dog. Make
up your own race. You can hop, skip
and jump. You can jog or sprint. Think
of different ways to move
your body!

It's important to be active all year. Is it snowing outside? Put on a coat and wrap up warm. It's time to go sledging!

In bad weather, be safe and exercise inside. Be active at home or find an indoor play space. Climb and play. Play tug-of-war. Don't let bad weather stop you from being active.

You can stay active by planning your day. Ask an adult to help you. Choose how you want to spend your free time. Be mindful of how much time you spend on **electronic devices**. Make sure you have time to exercise.

Take care of your body by staying active. Exercise keeps your whole body healthy. It gives you energy and keeps you fit. And it's lots of fun!

Glossary

balance to keep steady and not fall over

confidence a feeling or belief that you can do well

electronic device battery-powered object, such as a mobile phone, tablet, laptop or computer

flexible able to bend or move easily

focus to keep all your attention

goal something that you aim for or work towards

karate a martial art using controlled kicks and punches

posture the way in which your body is positioned when you are sitting or standing

scavenger hunt a game in which people look for hidden items

yoga exercises and ways of breathing that keep the mind and body healthy

Find out more

Feeling Good About Yourself (Ali and Annie's Guides), Jilly Hunt (Raintree, 2020)

I Stay Active (Healthy Me), Martha E. H. Rustad (Raintree, 2018)

Keeping Fit (Let's Read and Talk About), Honor Head (Franklin Watts, 2014)

Websites

www.nhs.uk/change4life
The Change4life website has lots of ideas to help you stay healthy.

**www.youtube.com/channel/
UCAxW1XT0iEJo0TYlRfn6rYQ**
Get fit with the nation's unofficial P.E. teacher, Joe Wicks.

Index